THE BATTLE OF GETTYSBURG

Essential Library

An Imprint of Abdo Publishing
abdopublishing.com

ESSENTIAL LIBRARY OF
★ THE CIVIL ★
WAR

BY TOM STREISSGUTH

CONTENT CONSULTANT

ERIK B. ALEXANDER
ASSISTANT PROFESSOR
SOUTHERN ILLINOIS UNIVERSITY EDWARDSVILLE

abdopublishing.com

Published by Abdo Publishing, a division of ABDO, PO Box 398166, Minneapolis, Minnesota 55439. Copyright © 2017 by Abdo Consulting Group, Inc. International copyrights reserved in all countries. No part of this book may be reproduced in any form without written permission from the publisher. Essential Library™ is a trademark and logo of Abdo Publishing.

Printed in the United States of America, North Mankato, Minnesota

052016
092016

Cover Photo: E. W. Kelley/Library of Congress
Interior Photos: E. W. Kelley/Library of Congress, 1; Library of Congress, 4, 15, 16, 22, 26, 36, 39, 43, 44, 49, 61, 69, 79, 89, 97, 98 (top); Ian Dagnall Computing/Alamy, 9; Kurz & Allison/Library of Congress, 11; Benjamin Lloyd Singley/Library of Congress, 19; Bettmann/Corbis, 31, 99 (top); Detroit Publishing Company/Library of Congress, 35, 55, 73; Conrad Freitag/Library of Congress, 50; Alexander Gardner/Library of Congress, 58; White Studio/Library of Congress, 64; Medford Historical Society/ Corbis, 68; Keystone View Company/Library of Congress, 70; Timothy H. O'Sullivan/Library of Congress, 80, 82, 93; Edwin Forbes/Library of Congress, 86, 98 (bottom); Delmas Lehman/iStockphoto/Thinkstock, 91, 99 (bottom)

Editor: Amanda Lanser
Series Designers: Kelsey Oseid and Maggie Villaume

Cataloging-in-Publication Data

Names: Streissguth, Tom, author.
Title: The Battle of Gettysburg / by Tom Streissguth.
Description: Minneapolis, MN : Abdo Publishing, [2017] | Series: Essential library
    of the Civil War | Includes bibliographical references and index.
Identifiers: LCCN 2015960302 | ISBN 9781680782738 (lib. bdg.) |
    ISBN 9781680774627 (ebook)
Subjects: LCSH: Gettysburg, Battle of, Gettysburg, Pa., 1863--Juvenile literature.
Classification: DDC 973.7/349--dc23
LC record available at http://lccn.loc.gov/2015960302

CONTENTS

Brigadier General John Buford faced a dilemma at the onset of the Civil War: on what side should he serve?

FIGHTING ON SEMINARY RIDGE

It was early in the morning of July 1, 1863. The sun rose over the hills lying west of the town of Gettysburg, Pennsylvania. From the high cupola of the Lutheran Seminary, Union brigadier general John Buford surveyed the fields and hills through his looking glass.

Born in the border state of Kentucky as the son of a slave owner, Buford had attended the US Military Academy at West Point. At the start of the Civil War in 1861, Buford had faced a difficult decision—one that many of his fellow army officers had faced as well. Should he join the Confederate States of America in rebellion against the United States? Or should he remain with the US Army and fight the rebels, some of whom were members of his own family?

Buford had decided to remain with the US Army, earning honors as a cavalry officer. He had arrived in Gettysburg in command of the US First Cavalry Division. Knowing the Confederate Army of Northern Virginia was in the area, he had sent out pickets north and west of town. Their dangerous job was to find and engage enemy scouts and screen the movement of their fellow soldiers.

When scattered fighting broke out, Buford sent a message to Major General John Reynolds, who commanded an entire wing—three infantry corps—of the Union army. Reynolds, who grew up just 50 miles (80 km) from Gettysburg, marched his infantry to Seminary Ridge. He deployed them in battle formation to meet the Confederates marching along the Chambersburg Pike.

As Buford strained to see through his spyglass, he heard shots ringing out west of town, and then a voice from the landing below the cupola.

"What's the matter, John?" said the voice. It was Reynolds.

"The devil's to pay!" replied Buford.[1] He climbed down to talk to Reynolds face-to-face. A skirmish between Union and Confederate troops was in progress on McPherson's Ridge, west of town. Several regiments of Union infantry, including the Second Wisconsin, were running toward the fighting on the hill.

The men of the Second Wisconsin were volunteers, as were most of the men of both armies. They wore tall, black hats and proudly carried eight regimental flags. After reaching McPherson's Ridge, they formed into lines two and three men deep to face the Confederates. Suddenly, a tremendous noise rang out. General James Archer's Confederate brigade had fired a powerful first volley into the Union lines. With no time to load their guns, the Wisconsin troops fixed bayonets to their rifles and charged the Confederates.

The men of the Confederate army prided themselves on their courage and fighting skill. If the numbers were equal, they believed they could soundly defeat any regiment in the Union army. But they were not prepared for this fearsome charge on McPherson's Ridge. Archer's men broke and fled to the rear. The Union troops swarming across the hill took General Archer prisoner.

Riding up behind the Second Wisconsin was John Reynolds and his infantry. He was eager to follow up the Second Wisconsin's success with an attack on Archer's other regiments to the west. Reynolds turned back toward Gettysburg

VICKSBURG AND GETTYSBURG

When the Confederates invaded Pennsylvania, their stronghold along the Mississippi River—Vicksburg, Mississippi—was under Union siege. Its fall would disrupt supplies and the movement of troops in the Confederate states. Confederate general Robert E. Lee believed attacking Pennsylvania would distract the Union army. If the Army of Northern Virginia could draw some of the Union forces at Vicksburg north to protect Pennsylvania, Vicksburg might be able to withstand the siege. As a result, the Union might negotiate an end to the war that allowed the Confederacy to survive. The Battles of Gettysburg and Vicksburg were decided within a day of each other—the Union had won both. The Union victories were a key turning point in the Civil War.

to see if reinforcements were on the way. A Confederate bullet struck him in the neck. Reynolds fell from his horse—dead. It was the first day of the Battle of Gettysburg.

HOW THE WAR BEGAN

The Civil War (1861–1865) began on April 12, 1861, with the bombardment of Fort Sumter in the harbor of Charleston, South Carolina. Several batteries of heavy guns under the command of Confederate brigadier general P. G. T. Beauregard opened fire on the Union fort. The bombardment continued until the afternoon of April 13, when the garrison surrendered. Major Robert Anderson, Sumter's commander, ordered an evacuation by the garrison on the next day.

South Carolina had declared its independence and seceded from the United States on December 20, 1860. By February 1, 1861, six other Southern states had done the same. Together, they formed the Confederate States of America. The people in these states saw the election of President Abraham Lincoln on November 6, 1860, as a threat to their freedom and to the institution of slavery, upon which the Southern economy relied. Lincoln's antislavery views were well known, and many Southern leaders believed he was prepared to ban slavery throughout the country. After the Battle of Fort Sumter, four more states joined the Confederacy.

The first major battle of the Civil War took place in July 1861, at Manassas in northern Virginia. It was called the Battle of Bull Run. The Confederate army outmaneuvered the Union troops and sent them in a panicked, headlong retreat. In 1862, the Union army was again thrown back after an assault on the Confederate capital of Richmond, Virginia.

By early 1863, the war had reached a stalemate in the eastern states, while Union armies advanced in the Mississippi River valley and Tennessee. The Union Army of the Potomac, under the command of General Joseph Hooker, protected Washington, DC, the federal capital. Hooker's army fought several battles against the Confederate Army of Northern Virginia, under General Robert E. Lee. Hooker's army was larger, but Lee was a brilliant and aggressive commander whose troops were intensely loyal to their leader and the Southern cause.

SURPRISE AT CHANCELLORSVILLE

It was early in the evening on May 2, 1863. The men of Union general Oliver O. Howard's XI Corps sat around their campfires. They were a mile (1.6 km) from the battlefront near Chancellorsville, Virginia, protecting the Union right flank that faced Confederate armies to the south. Many of the men believed the next day would bring some action. Then again, it might not. In a battle, the only thing that was routine was to be surprised by—and hopefully, prepared for—the unexpected.

This 1890 print shows the Confederate advance on Union troops.

On May 3, the sound of beating hooves reached the camp. General Howard's men looked up to see deer leaping through the forest toward them and rabbits scurrying along the ground. Then human yells pierced the quiet air.

Confederate troops in light gray uniforms burst from the forest, bayonets fixed to their rifles. Their commander, Thomas "Stonewall" Jackson, had marched 28,000 men 12 miles (19 km) completely around the Union lines.[2] General Lee had divided his forces in the midst of battle, keeping a much smaller force in front of the main body of the Union army. This would allow the rest of his troops to sneak around for a surprise attack. It was a very big risk that, if successful, would result in major victory.

Stonewall Jackson's Confederates achieved total surprise when they fell upon Howard's resting troops. Howard's troops scattered, as did the rest of the Union forces. The entire Union army was

DEATH BY OTHER MEANS

Shortly after the assault on Chancellorsville, Stonewall Jackson was wounded by a stray bullet fired by one of his own men. The victory and the battle would be his last. Jackson died as thousands of other Civil War soldiers did—from his medical care. He was immediately brought to a skilled surgeon. Before the wound could become infected, the surgeon followed standard procedure by amputating Jackson's left arm. Although he was a top-ranking officer, Jackson still had to survive the unsanitary conditions that prevailed in hospitals of his day. Scientists had not yet discovered that bacteria cause infection and disease, so surgeons and doctors did not wash their hands or their instruments. In addition, few pain medications were available. A few days after the operation, Jackson came down with pneumonia. He died of this contagious disease a week after being shot on the battlefield.

forced to retreat. Lee's risk paid off. The Battle of Chancellorsville was one of the Confederacy's most dramatic victories.

THE PLANNED INVASION

Success at Chancellorsville boosted the morale of the Army of Northern Virginia. It also inspired General Lee to plan an even riskier campaign for his troops. But the Southerners had also taken a very serious loss. On May 10, Stonewall Jackson died from wounds suffered in a friendly fire incident during the battle.

As the Union Army of the Potomac withdrew north of the Rappahannock River, Lee now had a chance to bring the war to Northern soil. He would march west to the Shenandoah Valley of western Virginia, then north to the Potomac River. He reorganized his army into three corps under the command of James Longstreet, A. P. Hill, and Richard S. Ewell.

The Potomac separated Virginia from Maryland, a Union border state where slavery remained legal and many residents sympathized with the Confederacy. The bloody Battle of Antietam had been fought in Maryland on September 17, 1862. Outnumbered, Lee fought the Union army to a standstill. But the bloodied Confederate army was forced back to Virginia, leaving thousands of dead and wounded behind.

Now the Confederates were returning to Union territory in even greater numbers, this time to Pennsylvania. Their goal was to strike and defeat the

Union army that would be sent north to stop them. They would threaten a crucial railroad bridge at Harrisburg, the capital of Pennsylvania, and menace civilians in the Pennsylvania countryside. By doing this, Lee believed he could force the Union to the bargaining table and negotiate an agreement that would end the war and preserve the independent Confederate States of America.

At the very least, by bringing his army north, Lee would bring his army to more bountiful ground. Two years of fighting had devastated the farms of northern Virginia. This battle-scarred land could no longer support Lee's hungry army. Instead, his soldiers would live off the fertile Pennsylvania countryside. Union supporters, instead of Southerners, would now witness firsthand the chaos and destruction of war.

In early 1863, the residents of Gettysburg, Pennsylvania, had not yet seen combat.

Brigadier General Joseph Hooker suffered defeat at the Battle of Chancellorsville.

CHAPTER

★ **2** ★

THE INVASION OF PENNSYLVANIA

Union brigadier general Joseph Hooker had lost his nerve at the Battle of Chancellorsville. When General Lee ordered a daring march by Stonewall Jackson's corps to surprise the Union army, Hooker panicked. The result was defeat on the battlefield and the loss of the respect of many of his staff officers. "He acts like a man without a plan," remarked General Marsena Patrick, a Union brigade commander. "He knows that Lee is his master, and is afraid to meet him in fair battle."[1]

On Lincoln's urging, Hooker finally moved his army out of its camp at Falmouth, Virginia, on June 10, 1863. The Army of the Potomac followed the Confederates through northern Virginia.

On June 15, the army reached Fairfax, just south of the Potomac River. Hooker sent a message to Washington, DC, demanding reinforcements. He wanted troops manning the forts guarding the capital to join the Army of the Potomac in Fairfax. Henry Halleck, general in chief of the US Army, agreed to release part of the Washington garrison to join Hooker's army.

HOOKER ARGUES

Meanwhile, General Lee's troops were marching through Maryland unopposed. As Lee brought his troops north across the Potomac River on June 15, Hooker kept his distance. A Confederate force had already captured the Virginian town of Winchester, which had been in Union hands. But a strong garrison of 10,000 Union troops still occupied Harpers Ferry, Virginia.[2] This town held an important strategic position at the confluence of the Shenandoah and Potomac Rivers. Hooker finally ordered the Army of the Potomac to follow Lee's army. Union troops were now directly between the Confederate army and Washington, DC.

Lincoln wanted Washington protected at all costs. But he also believed Hooker had the means to defeat Lee's army. Confederate supplies were getting low, and Lee's men were forced to move constantly to live off the land. But instead of advancing against Lee, Hooker asked for reinforcements, this time from the Harpers Ferry garrison. With Harpers Ferry now behind Confederate

Located at the junction of the Potomac and Shenandoah Rivers, Harpers Ferry

lines, Hooker believed these troops could better serve elsewhere. But Halleck disagreed, as did Lincoln. They did not want to surrender the town, now the last Union stronghold in western Virginia. General Hooker rode into Harpers Ferry, but the garrison commander had instructions from General Halleck to ignore any orders Hooker might give.

THE FENCES AT GETTYSBURG

As they entered Pennsylvania, Confederate soldiers saw something unfamiliar. The land was divided into many small plots of land marked off by fences. In the south, the use of slaves allowed much larger plantations to thrive, and in many places, fences were rare. The fences in the North would play a key role in the Battle of Gettysburg. They slowed down infantry and horses moving across open land. They also forced men climbing over them to rise in the air, making them vulnerable targets. Observers walking the fields near Gettysburg after the battle noticed many of the dead had fallen along the fence lines. The narrow lanes between the fences and the roads were used for dozens of mass graves.

Convinced Halleck and Lincoln were undermining him, Hooker fired off a message to Washington. Either he would be allowed to take command of the Harpers Ferry garrison, or he would quit.

In Lincoln's opinion, Hooker had a golden opportunity to outmaneuver General Lee. "We cannot help beating him," the president said, "if we have the man."[3] But Hooker seemed more eager to do battle with his superiors in Washington than with the Confederate army. On the same day he received Hooker's telegram, Lincoln accepted the general's resignation.

THE REBELS MARCH NORTH

Meanwhile, the Confederate army continued north. The infantry columns stretched for miles along narrow roads. A long train of supply wagons, guarded by men on horseback, brought up the rear.

Lee also gave important instructions to his cavalry commander, James Ewell Brown "Jeb" Stuart. The Confederate horsemen kept an eye on the Union troops. They also scouted the ground, guarded the right flank of General Ewell's corps, and gathered supplies as they could. Now that he was in enemy territory, Lee could no longer rely on civilian informants. He used Stuart's cavalry as his eyes and ears on the enemy.

To the civilians they passed, the Confederate army looked worn out and unkempt. One civilian noted, "Many were ragged, shoeless, and filthy [but] well armed, and under perfect discipline. They seemed to move as one vast machine."[4] Many Confederate soldiers marched with worn-out shoes or no shoes at all. Their clothing was stained and tattered. The men were hungry and thirsty and had been sleeping in the open for weeks. Yet their spirits were high, and they were confident a single great victory against the Army of the Potomac would end the war once and for all.

GEORGE GORDON MEADE

1815–1872

General George Gordon Meade took command of the Army of the Potomac just three days before the Battle of Gettysburg. Very few believed Meade capable of outsmarting and defeating Robert E. Lee, the best commander the Confederacy had. Not only did Meade manage it, but his victory at Gettysburg turned the tide of the Civil War in the east.

Born in Spain, Meade attended the US Military Academy at West Point. He graduated in 1835 but left the military soon after his required term of service ended. In 1842, he rejoined the army, serving as an engineer before the outbreak of the Civil War. Meade commanded a division at the Battle of Antietam in 1862.

In 1863, Meade was promoted to commander of the Union Army V Corps. He led the V at Chancellorsville, the Union defeat that ended the career of General Joseph Hooker. When Meade replaced Hooker as commander of the Army of the Potomac on June 28, 1863, he was hardly enthusiastic about his own promotion. Yet he skillfully defended Gettysburg, a place he had never seen before the battle, against Lee and a powerful Confederate army. After the battle, a monument to Meade was raised on Cemetery Ridge, showing Meade astride his horse, "Old Baldy."

MEADE TAKES COMMAND

After Hooker resigned, President Lincoln promoted General George Gordon Meade as the new commander of the Army of the Potomac. Meade was the fourth commander of the army appointed within a year.

The promotion surprised many Union officers, several of whom held a higher rank than Meade. The new commander could be cold and distant to his fellow officers, and he was often in a foul temper. Nevertheless, Meade was now responsible for leading the seven corps of the army, along with its artillery batteries and cavalry brigades, and for stopping Lee's advance into Pennsylvania.

Meade understood the situation in Pennsylvania was urgent. He quickly gave instructions and orders to the corps commanders in Maryland. He had two divisions of Union cavalry positioned to the west between the main Union army and the route Lee's Confederates took through northwest Maryland. He ordered

FOR WANT OF A MAP

Lee, Meade, and other Civil War commanders often lacked detailed maps of the fields, rivers, and mountains where they fought. In the nineteenth century, maps were hard to find and often inaccurate. "The average citizen today," writes historian Michael Korda, "with a road map or, more likely, a cell phone and a GPS navigation device in his or her car, would be better informed than was either commanding general [at Gettysburg]. . . . In Pennsylvania, enemy territory, Lee was on his own; he had little idea of what was in front of him."[5]

two corps and a cavalry unit north to Emmitsburg, Maryland, just south of the Pennsylvania state line, and four to Taneytown, to the northeast.

A driving rain had been falling for several days, turning the roads to mud and making life miserable for Meade's troops. Many of Meade's own officers felt their leader was ordering marches without any purpose or goal. Many also suspected him of cowardice. They believed he was unwilling to take the war to the Confederates.

BUILDING A CIVIL WAR ARMY

The Union and Confederate armies shared the same basic organization. Men volunteering for service were organized into regiments commanded by colonels. These regiments included up to 1,000 men and were named after their state of origin.[6] The Twenty-Eighth New York, for example, means the twenty-eighth regiment of volunteers organized in that state. Several regiments were gathered into a single brigade under the command of a brigadier general. In turn, two or more brigades made up a division, and two or more divisions were included in a corps. Cavalry was organized in brigades and divisions as well.

The basic unit of artillery was the battery—a collection of four or six big guns, which could move independently or be assigned to support an infantry division or brigade. Artillery guns included smoothbore cannon, howitzers, Parrott rifles, and Napoleons, the last of which was named for an emperor of France. Civil War artillery fired explosive shells; iron shot; canister, which exploded with a deadly hail of small pellets; or case shot, which contained small musket balls.

THE GENERAL AND THE SPY

On the Confederate side, General Longstreet had, at first, favored sending the Confederate army west to Tennessee to engage the Union army under the command of General Ulysses S. Grant. But Lee persuaded him that an invasion of Pennsylvania might draw the Army of the Potomac into a decisive battle. When he realized Lee was determined to press ahead, Longstreet immediately put in a request to Richmond for a supply of gold coins. He turned the money over to his trusted spy, Henry Thomas Harrison.

Longstreet instructed Harrison to travel to Washington, DC, and report on anything he heard about the Army of the Potomac. Though General Lee did not like using spies, Longstreet felt no such hesitation. The Confederate army needed all the information it could get.

Longstreet and Lee were growing frustrated from the lack of communication from cavalry commander Stuart. The Confederate cavalry were out of touch, ranging far to the east. They were out of contact with the Union forces as well, and seemed to have taken leave altogether from the Pennsylvania campaign. Lee trusted Stuart as an old friend and a capable commander. But Stuart also had an independent streak, which would have a very serious impact on Lee's ability to wage war in Pennsylvania.

CHAPTER

★ 3 ★

THE CONFEDERATES ARRIVE

The farmers and townspeople of Maryland and southern Pennsylvania watched the Confederate armies pass. Many families loaded up their wagons and fled, crowding the roads to Philadelphia and points east. But some gathered their weapons and raised barricades in the streets. In Maryland, the residents of Baltimore put out small barrels filled with sand to block the streets.

Lee's army slogged along the muddy country lanes. There had been several days of rain. The men took to the neighboring fields when the roads became impassable. They trampled down crops that had been planted just a few weeks earlier. In the rear was a smaller army of cooks, drivers, and laborers, most of them slaves brought north. When Confederate troops came across African Americans in the North, they took prisoners. Whether or not they were free persons of color, they were valuable and could be sold at Southern slave markets.

Before arriving in Pennsylvania, General Lee issued strict orders. He wanted no thieving, looting, or assaults on white civilians. The soldiers were to pay for any goods they took. Lee believed he could turn the Northerners against the war by keeping his army in check. But he did not take into account the amount of food his army needed or that most of his officers and enlisted men had very little real money—gold or silver coins—with them.

THE KNIGHTS DESCEND ON GETTYSBURG

Several con men took advantage of the Confederate invasion to ply their trade among the trusting farmers and townspeople of Pennsylvania. Riding ahead of Lee's army, they represented themselves as agents of a secret society, the Knights of the Golden Circle. Based in the South, this society really existed, and was known to the Pennsylvanians and other Union citizens. For a dollar, the Knights offered memberships to the local farmers and townspeople. The swindlers would then show the secret signs and handshakes that, according to them, would give the new members protection against any damage or injury from the Southerners. The Northern "Knights" gave Confederate soldiers these secret—and phony—signs as the Southern troops marched through the Pennsylvania countryside.

AN EASY VICTORY

Confederate general Ewell's corps followed the Cumberland Valley north into Pennsylvania. A division under Jubal Early split off and headed straight east for York and the Susquehanna River valley. Their route to the river took them through Gettysburg, a small crossroads town surrounded by farms and forested hills.

On June 26, the Union Twenty-Sixth Pennsylvania Militia under Major Granville Haller marched to meet Early's division. After he got word the Twenty-Sixth Pennsylvania was blocking the road to Gettysburg, Early sent a brigade of cavalry to the north. The cavalry would attack from that direction, while an infantry division under John Brown Gordon would advance directly east against the Pennsylvanians.

YORK'S STORES

On June 28, Early's division approached the town of York, which was defended by a small local militia. As the Confederates marched upon York, a committee of townspeople came out and announced their surrender. Early called a meeting at the courthouse and laid out his demands: thousands of barrels of flour, sugar, and molasses; 32,000 pounds (14,500 kg) of meat; and 2,000 pairs of shoes or boots, as well as socks and $100,000 in cash. After collecting the contribution, which included only about $28,000 of the demanded money, Early pressed on toward Harrisburg.

The Union militia took up a defensive position behind Marsh Creek, a few miles from the center of Gettysburg. Many of these Pennsylvania men had no military experience. One of the militia companies was made up of students from Pennsylvania College. Other companies had only been in uniform a few days. Forming a line parallel to the creek, they readied their weapons.

Gordon's infantry advanced, firing off a volley. Hundreds of muzzle flashes and a deafening roar signaled the arrival of the Confederate army on the outskirts of Gettysburg. After trading a few volleys with the rebels, the Union militia broke formation and ran. Some hurried aboard trains in Gettysburg headed east. Others threw off their uniforms and made for their homes. The skirmish had lasted just a few minutes.

A CHANGE OF BATTLE PLANS

Later that afternoon, Early's division marched into Gettysburg. But the town was not a military objective, and Lee had no intention of holding it. The goal was Harrisburg, the state capital. Early's orders were to continue moving east to the city of York and the Susquehanna River. From there, he would drive north to Harrisburg.

Meanwhile, Henry Thomas Harrison, General Longstreet's spy, had returned from Washington. He brought the news that George Meade had replaced Joseph Hooker as commander of the Army of the Potomac. Harrison also revealed that the Union troops were still widely separated in northern Maryland, but they were marching north into Pennsylvania in pursuit of the Confederates.

Though General Lee did not favor using spies, General Longstreet and reports from other sources convinced him the Union army was still scattered around the Maryland countryside. As the new head of the Union army, Meade likely had little direct control over his corps commanders. This would make the Union forces easy prey, Lee believed, if he could quickly pull the Confederate army together.

Lee would no longer wait for the Union to move north to Harrisburg. He would amass his army, search out Meade's corps, and destroy them one by one. He ordered Early and Ewell to march back toward Gettysburg. Lee wanted to gather his forces near the crossroads town and strike Meade while the Union army was still vulnerable.

One serious problem remained: the whereabouts of Jeb Stuart and the Confederate cavalry. Stuart was still riding through Maryland between the Union army and Washington. Reading Lee's instructions, Stuart assumed his mission was to scout the Union lines and gather supplies where he could. But in fact, Lee expected Stuart to guard the right flank of General Ewell's corps, much farther north. As an important battle loomed, Lee had a single question in mind: Where was Stuart?

MEADE PREPARES

Union general Meade was a cautious commander. He felt unprepared for the responsibility Lincoln had placed on his shoulders. Short-tempered and often reserved, Meade was not popular among the division and brigade officers who now served under him. But he was capable of making hard decisions when necessary. He had long experience in military tactics and strategy and knew how to deploy large infantry units effectively.

THE BLUE AND THE BUTTERNUT

The appearance of Confederate soldiers—particularly their clothing—surprised many Pennsylvania civilians during Lee's advance. It was well known that Union troops wore blue uniforms and the Southerners wore gray. But these troops had tunics that appeared light tan or khaki-colored. Although the fabric was originally gray, the cheap dye used to tint the uniforms soon faded to butternut, a name inspired by the homemade cloth dyed with the bark from the butternut tree.

Meade ordered the I Corps, under the command of John Reynolds, and the XI Corps, under the command of Oliver Howard, to march north. Their mission was to search for Confederate units along the road to Gettysburg. The III Corps would stay in Emmitsburg, Maryland, just south of the Pennsylvania state line.

On June 30, Meade learned Lee was moving back toward Gettysburg. Meade believed Lee was going to strike at the Union army as soon as he could. To meet the assault, he prepared a defensive line running east and west along Pipe Creek, in northern Maryland.

Here, Meade believed, he would be able to make a strong stand against Lee's army, which was heading to meet the Army of the Potomac. But one of his commanders thought differently. Although Meade had ordered Reynolds to retreat south if he should encounter any Confederates, Reynolds had no intention of following this order. He would bring his I Corps to Gettysburg, along with the XI Corps right behind him. Along the way, his divisions would smash the Confederates wherever they may find them.

Before the war, Meade sought to avoid any division of the country over slavery. In the army, he had several rivals among men who supported the abolition of slavery and total war against the South. Several Union commanders, not seeing eye-to-eye with Meade, treated their commander's orders as suggestions and handled their units as they saw fit. On the first day of the Battle of Gettysburg, Meade found that John Buford, John Reynolds, and Oliver Howard were seeking out a fight near Gettysburg—despite Meade's plan to keep the army in Maryland. As a result, when the battle finally broke out, Meade had no choice but to bring up the rest of his army.

MAJOR GENERAL
JOHN FULTON REYNOLDS
UNITED STATES VOLUNTEERS

KEEP
OFF THIS MOUND

THE DAY BEFORE GETTYSBURG

Jeb Stuart believed in the romantic traditions of cavalry. He saw himself and his men as brave heroes on horseback who were a cut above the average infantryman. In Stuart's eyes, a cavalry soldier was a man of skill, valor, and courage. In his own opinion, Stuart himself was the best cavalry leader in either army.

But in the Civil War, massed infantry formations and artillery could fire devastating volleys from high ground or dug-in positions. This made traditional cavalry charges in the midst of larger battles obsolete. Cavalry brigades still had important roles to play. They could serve as scouts or pickets driving on an enemy's flanks in battle. Cavalry could also serve to disrupt and terrify enemy civilians. As raiders, mounted soldiers could move freely through the countryside, seizing needed supplies and goods.

THE EQUINE DEAD

By one estimate, 3,000 horses died at Gettysburg.[1] While Civil War armies moved on foot, cavalry units and artillery batteries used horses and mules. The battle would take a heavy toll on these draft animals as well as on humans. Horses made large targets, and they could not shoot back. When disabled, they were simply shot. The carcasses were a big problem for civilians, since military burial details usually did not bother with animals. The widow Lydia Leister had the honor of seeing her home on Cemetery Ridge used by General Meade as a temporary headquarters. She fled as the battle commenced, but when she returned on July 4, the day after the battle, she found 17 dead horses lying in her front yard.

Stuart was a proud officer who also had a grudge against his Union foes. At the Battle of Brandy Station, shortly after Chancellorsville, the Union cavalry brigades under General John Buford had fought the rebel horsemen to a draw. The largest cavalry battle of the Civil War, Brandy Station proved Northerners could fight as well on horseback as Confederates could. For Stuart, this posed a slight on his own reputation—one he was determined to revenge.

CONFEDERATES CONVERGE ON GETTYSBURG

Under Lee's orders to gather with the other two Confederate corps, General A. P. Hill marched his own Third Corps east to Cashtown, approximately eight miles (13 km) from Gettysburg. Behind him was General Longstreet. Together with

Confederate general James Longstreet commanded a corps at Gettysburg.

Ewell, Hill and Longstreet commanded three full corps of Confederate troops, including infantry and artillery.

THE ARMIES COLLIDE

Dr. E. B. Spence, a Confederate surgeon, and the spy Henry Harrison were in Gettysburg on the morning of June 30. They spotted Union troops moving north and rushed back to report to Henry Heth, one of Hill's division commanders. They were the first to see the troops of Reynolds's I Corps approaching from the south. Heth could also hear drums coming from south of Gettysburg. For signaling purposes, cavalry used bugles and infantry used drummers while marching. Heth knew there was a good chance Hill's corps now faced much more than cavalry pickets.

To further scope out the countryside, Hill decided to send infantry forward toward Gettysburg. On June 30, Heth reported a rumor that a good supply of shoes—which his infantry desperately needed—could be found in the town. He asked permission to move out and retrieve them.

Hill did not realize what was facing the Confederates in Gettysburg. "The only force in Gettysburg is cavalry, probably a detachment of observation," he replied to Heth.[2] He ordered Heth to lead a reconnaissance to Gettysburg on the next day, July 1. When Heth arrived, he was to requisition the badly needed footwear and any other supplies available for his troops.

Hill did not believe Meade could have infantry in Gettysburg this quickly. He believed the main Union army must still be camped in Maryland. However, Lee's instructions required Hill to move his corps through Gettysburg the next day. There could be fighting, so the general ordered a draught of whiskey to each of the men in his corps.

WOMEN IN BATTLE

Women were barred from military service on both Union and Confederate sides. But that did not stop at least seven women from fighting in disguise at Gettysburg. Two women fought for the Union, both of whom survived the battle. On the Confederate side, five female soldiers have been discovered. One was wounded on the battlefield and later lost her leg in a Pennsylvania hospital.

Thomas Reed, a Union soldier in the same hospital, described her in a letter home: "I must tell you that we have a female Secesh [Confederate soldier] here. She was wounded at Gettysburg but our doctors soon found her out."[3] Two other women fighting for the Confederacy were killed on the third day of battle.

BUFORD'S CAVALRY

Meanwhile, Union cavalry commander John Buford sent his pickets ahead. The Union cavalry spread out west, north, and east of Gettysburg. These pickets were used for scouting and skirmishing with the enemy cavalry. When faced with a big infantry regiment, they scattered. Cavalry troops were not trained for fighting on foot or forming up a line of battle. But the Union cavalry did have one advantage: their Spencer carbines. These new rifles could fire up to 20 rounds a minute, the quickest rate of any small gun in the Civil War.

Another effective Union weapon was Buford himself, a hard-fighting, aggressive commander. At Gettysburg, he believed his cavalry had a fine opportunity. Lee's army was marching in enemy territory and spread out on unfamiliar roads. It could be attacked piece by piece. If Buford could sow confusion among them, the Confederates would be easy prey for the Union's seven corps of infantry.

But Meade was not so sure. Gettysburg and southern Pennsylvania were unfamiliar territory to him as well. A defensive position in northern Maryland satisfied him, for now. To his corps commanders, he wrote: "The commanding general is satisfied that the object of the movement of the army has been accomplished. . . . It is no longer his intention to assume the offensive until . . . certain of success."[4]

But on the evening of June 30, Meade would get information that would force him into battle. One of Buford's horsemen had captured a Confederate trooper north of town. The prisoner belonged to Ewell's corps, and revealed that his unit was approaching from the north. A local farmer also came through the lines to warn Union officers a Confederate army was on the march.

Two armies were now on a collision course. They would meet somewhere near a small, peaceful Pennsylvania crossroads town. Both General Lee and General Meade realized the outcome of this fight could decide the entire war.

HAUNTED GETTYSBURG

As the site of one of the deadliest battles in history, Gettysburg has inspired many supernatural legends and rumors since 1863. Gettysburg College, which was Pennsylvania College at the time of the fight, is said to contain the ghosts of soldiers who were brought in wounded and soon died. Phantom footsteps and voices are said to be heard in many private homes scattered around the battlefield.

The cupola of the Lutheran Seminary had a commanding view of the battlefield.

THE FIRST DAY OF GETTYSBURG

On July 1, Confederate commander Henry Heth sent two brigades of infantry east toward Gettysburg. The Confederate troops passed fenced pastures, woodlots, fields, and a small stream called Marsh Creek. They knew Union troops were waiting for them in and around Gettysburg.

As they crested a hill, the Confederates spotted enemy skirmishers in front. Brigadier General James Archer's men at the front of the Confederate column formed a line of battle. Marching in two parallel ranks, they moved out on both sides of the road, their lines facing east.

Meanwhile, John Buford climbed the cupola of Gettysburg's Lutheran Seminary to have a look westward. In the distance, he could see Heth's infantry brigades advancing directly toward him. Realizing a battle was about to begin, Buford ordered two brigades of cavalry forward to take up defensive positions along McPherson's Ridge to the west.

When they reached the hill, the Union cavalry dismounted. Every fourth man was needed to hold the horses during the battle. The skirmishers pressed forward, their rapid-fire Spencer carbines spitting bullets at the Confederate lines.

Heth's men responded with roaring volleys from their single-shot rifles. Both sides readied artillery and trained the heavy guns across the open ground.

OPENING THE BALL

At approximately 7:30 a.m. on July 1, Lieutenant Marcellus Jones of the Union's Eighth Illinois Cavalry and his three companions were on a scouting mission. They had just spotted a long line of Confederate troops. The Illinois scouts were under orders to ride ahead of the main cavalry force. If they spotted the enemy, they were to report back on the double. On this particular day, however, a routine assignment was not enough for Jones. When the Confederates were seen, one of his men raised his gun. "Hold on," said Jones. "Give me the honor of opening this ball."[1] Borrowing a rapid-fire Spencer carbine, Jones steadied the gun on a fence. He took aim at a mounted Confederate officer 700 yards (600 m) away and fired. It was the first shot of the Battle of Gettysburg.

Shells screamed through the air and began exploding among the Confederate lines. Buford's goal was to hold the high ground around the seminary—Seminary Ridge—and delay the enemy just long enough for General Reynolds to bring up reinforcements from his I Corps.

REYNOLDS ARRIVES

Reynolds and the I Corps came up on horseback, reaching the seminary just as the Confederates were driving back Buford's cavalry. The noise of rifles and cannons rang in the distance, and smoke drifted across the fields. Reynolds immediately sent a messenger back to General Meade, explaining that a fight with Confederate infantry had broken out west of Gettysburg. His men would hold them off for as long as possible, but he was outnumbered. Meade must advance and send up the rest of the army. If the Confederates captured Gettysburg, they would have an open path to Cemetery Ridge, high ground that rose south of the town.

Buford and Reynolds would not have long to wait. Brigadier General Lysander Cutler's brigade was marching north to Seminary Ridge, as was the Iron Brigade, commanded by Solomon Meredith. These five regiments of tough, battle-hardened soldiers from Wisconsin, Michigan, and Indiana left the roads that led directly to Gettysburg. They hurried across the open fields toward the sound of rifle fire, knocking down rail fences in their way.

GETTYSBURG BATTLE MAP

The Battle of Gettysburg covered 25 square miles (65 sq km) around the town of Gettysburg, Pennsylvania. Both the Confederate and Union armies used roads, buildings, and natural features around the town to gain an advantage in battle.

On June 30, the day before battle, the Confederate army was largely in Cashtown, northwest of Gettysburg. Union general Reynolds marched his troops up to Gettysburg from the south, while Union cavalry pickets were north, west, and east of town. The battle started when these troops converged on Gettysburg on July 1. Fighting occurred all around the town of Gettysburg as residents looked on from their homes.

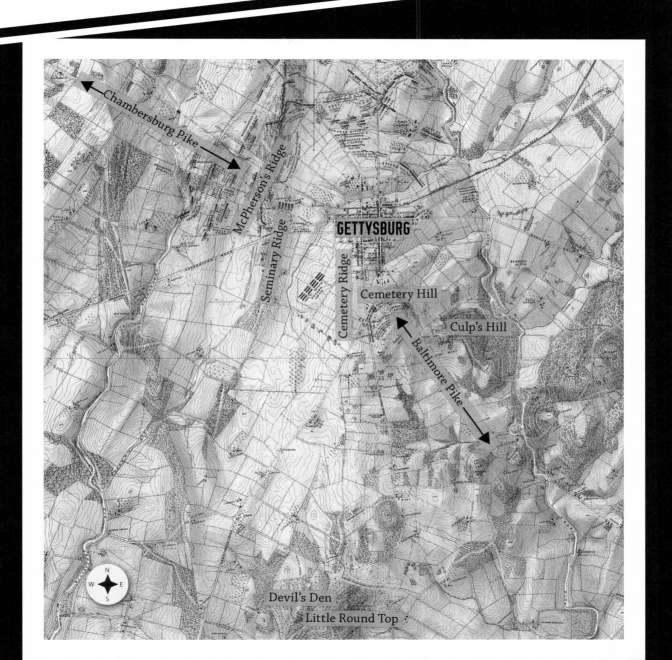

Chambersburg Pike

McPherson's Ridge

Seminary Ridge

GETTYSBURG

Cemetery Ridge

Cemetery Hill

Culp's Hill

Baltimore Pike

Devil's Den

Little Round Top

N
W   E
S

The Iron Brigade captures Confederate troops on July 1.

Reynolds divided his units, sending Cutler's brigade north of the seminary, while the Iron Brigade took up position just west of the building. At this point, the Confederate skirmishers were advancing east toward the Union lines.

The thickly wooded land began to rise, forcing the Confederates to advance uphill on unfamiliar ground.

With no time to load their rifles, the men of the Iron Brigade made for the cover of Herbst Woods, just west of Seminary Ridge. They formed lines of battle and fixed bayonets to their rifles. Reynolds and his aides rushed up to the lines, shouting encouragement. The chaotic fighting for the hilly woods between the Union Iron Brigade and Archer's Confederate brigade would leave hundreds of dead and wounded men on the ground.

Reynolds turned back to look for additional reinforcements, which should have been following behind Meredith's men. Just then, a Confederate sharpshooter took aim and a bullet struck Reynolds in the head. Reynolds fell from his horse—dead. Abner Doubleday of New York, the senior officer after Reynolds in the I Corps, took command.

Two Tennessee regiments advanced up the hill against the Sixth Wisconsin, letting off a deafening volley and killing or wounding dozens of the Union troops. Another Wisconsin regiment then appeared on the slope with fixed bayonets, charging toward the Confederate lines. The Iron Brigade's Indiana and Michigan regiments maneuvered around the Confederate right flank, forcing the Southerners to turn their line and then retreat back down the hill. Surrounded by Union troops, General Archer was taken prisoner.

THE TIDE OF BATTLE TURNS

Union troops carried Reynolds's body to the rear on an improvised stretcher. Soon afterward, Union general Oliver Howard arrived on the outskirts of Gettysburg at the head of the XI Corps. The battle along McPherson's Ridge and in the Herbst Woods had died down. Stunned and exhausted by the fighting, men from both sides retreated to wait for reinforcements. Doubleday ordered his troops to form a defensive line along Seminary Ridge and another hill, Oak Ridge, to the north.

Howard had spied Union troops retreating from Seminary Ridge. He believed the I Corps had suffered a serious setback. He sent a message to Meade, asking for reinforcements as soon as possible. Outranking Doubleday, Howard then took command of the troops on the battlefield.

Howard ordered Carl Schurz to take command of the I Corps and lead his troops north of Gettysburg. Schurz's mission was to head off Ewell's corps, which was approaching from the north, and to reinforce the right flank of the Union I Corps. Howard also sent a full division to take up a position on Cemetery Hill south of town. This division was to serve as a temporary reserve in case any part of the Union line was threatened with a Confederate breakthrough.

In the meantime, Confederate commander Hill sent reinforcements east as Ewell's corps arrived from the north. With these new units coming on the battlefield, the Union army faced a serious disadvantage. Arriving on horseback, General Lee rode forward toward the sound of artillery coming from the direction of Gettysburg.

Under Lee's urging, Hill and Heth renewed their attack on McPherson Ridge with two fresh brigades. The Iron Brigade fought at close quarters with a brigade of North Carolina regiments. At some points, the lines were fighting at a range of just 20 yards (18 m). Losses were heavy on both sides, with the Twenty-Fourth Michigan suffering a staggering casualty rate of 73 percent.[2] The commander of the Twenty-Sixth North Carolina was shot dead in the regiment's last charge against the Union troops.

JOHN BURNS JOINS THE FIGHT

At age 69, Gettysburg resident John Burns was a proud veteran of the War of 1812. When the first day's fighting broke out near his home, he ran directly toward the fighting. The commander of the 150th Pennsylvania suggested Burns head for the McPherson farm, where the Iron Brigade was facing several Confederate regiments at close range. Colonel John Callis of the Seventh Wisconsin allowed Burns to stay and fight. A sergeant handed Burns a captured Confederate rifle and sent him forward. As the battle grew hot near the McPherson farm, Burns was wounded three times and taken prisoner. Eventually, he was released and returned home. Burns became a hero for his day of service at Gettysburg and was personally congratulated by President Lincoln at the dedication of the national cemetery in November 1863.

GENERAL HANCOCK SCOUTS THE FIELD

Getting word that the I Corps was already skirmishing with the Confederates, General Meade realized a major fight was brewing in Gettysburg. Riding forward to investigate, Major General Winfield Hancock found a long, high ridge running two miles (3 km) south from Gettysburg, ending in two small hills: Round Top and Little Round Top. If Meade's remaining corps could take and hold Cemetery Ridge, they would have an excellent defensive position.

Meanwhile, north of Gettysburg, Richard Ewell's corps had arrived. Ewell sent a full division to hit the Union I Corps division commanded by General John Robinson at Oak Ridge. The Union troops took up a position behind a long stone wall. Robinson shifted his regiments around to bring fresh troops in to face the repeated Confederate assaults. To avoid being surrounded, the Union regiments eventually retreated from Oak Ridge. Holding out until the last, several hundred soldiers in the Sixteenth Maine were taken prisoner.

Thousands of men were retreating in disorder toward Gettysburg. The Confederates followed them. Soon the streets of the town were a scene of chaos and panic. Civilians watched from windows and alleys as men fought and died in the streets. In midafternoon, Confederate commander Jubal Early's division arrived from the east. Early's artillery commander set up his guns to sweep the wobbling Union lines.

Doubleday's division was also withering under waves of Confederate troops. Although the Union regiments threw up fence post barriers on Seminary Ridge, they were outnumbered. Late in the afternoon, Doubleday pulled his troops back to Cemetery Hill.

EWELL STANDS DOWN

With the Confederates chasing the beaten Union troops through Gettysburg, Lee saw an opportunity to take the high ground lying south of town. He gave instructions to General Ewell to capture Culp's Hill, which lay just to the east of Cemetery Hill, and drive the Union troops from these heights "if practicable."[3]

A SCHOOL DAY TO REMEMBER

The Battle of Gettysburg began on a Wednesday morning. At the time of the Civil War, there was no summer vacation, and classes were in session. At the Lutheran Seminary, the sound of rifle shots and artillery fire drowned out the professors. It gradually grew louder—and closer. Students rushed from their desks. Some ran out of the building to get a better look. At Pennsylvania College, students climbed to the top of Pennsylvania Hall to watch the fighting.

Down below, they could see big Union guns wheeling into position. A Confederate shell sailed overhead, but failed to explode on landing. The students rushed back down the stairs. Soldiers in blue uniforms were filling the stairways and heading for the roof. One teacher, in the middle of his reading, simply gave up. The teacher announced: "We will close and see what is going on, for you know nothing about the lesson anyhow."[4] Class was dismissed.

The polite wording of the message convinced Ewell that Lee was suggesting, not ordering. In Ewell's opinion, the final decision to attack was up to him. Believing the Union army was reinforcing its position, Ewell felt that an evening assault would be too risky. He held his men back.

The Confederates now controlled some hard-fought territory as well as the town of Gettysburg, but the heavy fighting had taken a toll on their numbers. The Union army now held two hills south of Gettysburg that would challenge any attacker. The rest of the Union army was approaching from Maryland with General Meade in command. Nevertheless, after the victory of July 1, General Lee would not retreat. There would be more fighting tomorrow.

CHAPTER

★ 6 ★

THE SECOND DAY OF BATTLE

The morning of July 2 dawned at Gettysburg. Pushed back by the Confederate regiments under the command of Richard Ewell and A. P. Hill, the outnumbered Union troops had retreated to the high ground of Cemetery Hill and Cemetery Ridge south of town. The town of Gettysburg was now in the hands of the Confederate army.

Instead of remaining in Maryland, General George Meade decided to send his remaining five corps north. As these troops arrived along the Baltimore Pike, they lined up on Cemetery Ridge, facing west over a patchwork of fenced fields and orchards, and at Cemetery Hill and Culp's Hill, facing Gettysburg to the north.

Artillery batteries took their place on the slopes of the hill and prepared for the expected Confederate advance.

Lee wanted to press the attack to catch the Union army while it was still weak and disorganized. He ordered General Longstreet to bring his corps south, facing the Union's left flank. Longstreet was to attack from the south, roll up the Union line, and drive Meade's troops off Cemetery Ridge.

Hill's corps were to keep the Union troops occupied in the center of the battlefield. Lee ordered Hill to bring his troops forward and threaten an attack. This would prevent Meade from pulling his troops out of this part of the line to reinforce his right flank. General Ewell, at the northern end of the Confederate line, was to capture the high ground on Cemetery Hill and Culp's Hill, if possible. In Lee's plan, Ewell and Longstreet would attack from north and south simultaneously. Unprepared for the assault and pressed from both directions, the Union army would be forced to retreat.

CONFUSION IN THE CONFEDERATE ARMY

Lee's battle plan did not account for confusion among his corps and division commanders. Richard Anderson commanded a division of five brigades. Marching behind the rest of Hill's corps, Anderson's division had not reached the battlefield on the first day. This may have cost the Confederates the best chance they had to seize Cemetery Hill on July 1.

General Ewell hoped to capture Culp's Hill for the Confederates.

As his division approached the center of the battlefield on July 2, Anderson found himself in a difficult situation between Hill and Longstreet, who were not on friendly terms. After Chancellorsville, Lee had transferred Anderson to Hill's corps. Now, with Longstreet leading the charge against the Union army, Longstreet and Hill failed to cooperate in planning Anderson's advance. The result was an uncoordinated attack in the center and right. Instead of taking Meade's army by surprise, the Confederates would face a solid line of Union troops ready and able to defend the high ground.

Anderson brought his brigades into formation in the open fields about a mile west of Cemetery Ridge. On the Union side, Hancock and the II Corps arrived on Cemetery Ridge between the IX Corps led by Colonel Adin Ballou Underwood on the right and Dan Sickles with the III Corps on the left. Through the morning and early afternoon of July 2, the Union army reinforced its lines on the hill. Meanwhile, the Confederate regiments maneuvered

THE SCANDALOUS DAN SICKLES

Commander Sickles had a talent for scandal. He was a favorite topic of gossip in New York, and his name was frequently in the newspapers. During a visit to England, he shocked Queen Victoria by introducing her to his mistress. He was also famous for shooting Phillip Barton Key, the son of Francis Scott Key, author of the "Star-Spangled Banner." Arrested and charged with murder, Sickles claimed jealousy over Key's interest in Sickles' wife, Theresa Bagioli, had made him crazy. He gained widespread sympathy during the trial and was the first murder suspect in the United States to win acquittal on the grounds of temporary insanity.

in the open for position. The day was hot, and men on both sides were thirsty and exhausted.

Sickles was a politician from New York. Despite his experience raising and training volunteers, General Meade saw him as an amateur and looked on him with contempt. On July 2, Meade instructed Sickles to take his corps of 10,000 men to a relatively safe position at the southern end of Cemetery Ridge and stay put.[1] Although Sickles had very little battlefield experience, he was an aggressive commander. He believed Meade was purposefully shunting him away from the action.

In front of Sickles's corps was a rise of ground surrounding a small peach orchard. Sickles was certain that if he did not seize this elevation, the Confederates would do so, giving them an advantage in the coming battle. Without informing General Meade or General Hancock, whose corps sat to his right, Sickles ordered his men forward. Unsupported by Hancock's troops, the III Corps advanced on the peach orchard, leaving a wide gap in the Union line.

FIGHTING IN THE PEACH ORCHARD

As the III Corps advanced into the open, General Lee saw his opportunity. Rather than attack from the south, Lee ordered Longstreet to move his divisions directly east against Sickles. The Confederate assault flooded over the peach orchard and a nearby stretch of uneven, rocky ground known as the Devil's Den.

Men investigate dead soldiers near Devil's Den near the peach orchard.

The volleys from the Confederate lines devastated the Union regiments, which took hundreds of casualties in a matter of minutes. A Confederate shell shattered Sickles's right leg. As Sickles was carried from the battlefield, Meade placed Hancock in command of the II and III Corps.

The Confederate brigades attacked the Union flanks from the south. In the peach orchard, the two lines fought at a distance of just a few dozen yards, and in some places soldiers fought hand-to-hand. The III Corps broke up into small groups of fighting, dying, and retreating men. At the same time, Union artillery positioned on Cemetery Ridge pounded the Confederates. Shells screamed overhead while the deadly shrapnel from canister shells tore the bodies of men and horses to pieces.

The Confederate advance demolished the III Corps and pushed the Union lines back. But Richard Anderson's division, used as a reserve at the start of the assault, failed to move into position to press the advantage. There was confusion as conflicting orders reached Anderson's brigade commanders.

Hancock attempted to reorganize his regiments, but hundreds of his men had been killed and wounded, and he only had 300 effective soldiers left on the battlefield.[2] Needing reinforcements immediately, he sent a call down the Union lines. The First Minnesota under James Colville came up in support, advancing into a streambed in the face of heavy Confederate fire.

The regiment bought the Union troops fighting south of Gettysburg time to regroup. But the fierce, close-range fighting decimated the First Minnesota, which suffered approximately 80 percent casualties. However, the Confederate advance also stalled, and Longstreet began withdrawing his exhausted Confederates from the front.

A BATTLE BREAK

The soldiers of the Fourth Alabama had been marching, fighting, and sweating for hours. Then came the hard part: storming uphill against Union troops on Little Round Top. They were tough veterans, but even these Alabamans could only bear so much physical hardship. "When we arrived there many of our poor fellows were . . . overcome with heat and weariness. . . . The men in line felt that they must lie down and rest awhile before making that second climb and storming the enemy's position on the crest. Thus our line stopped its advance, lay down among the rocks and [boulders], and simply returned the fire of the enemy . . . while the leaden hailstorm poured down upon us and filled my eyes with grit and gravel knocked off the big rocks about me. Fate was against us there."[3]

HOLDING LITTLE ROUND TOP

Farther south, a hill known as Little Round Top rose just south of Cemetery Ridge. Local farmers had cleared timber from the west side of this hill, making it an ideal position for massed artillery. From the boulder-strewn top of Little Round Top, artillerymen who managed to wrestle their guns up the narrow dirt trails could sweep the southern end of the battlefield.

Around half past four in the afternoon, realizing the Union army had not yet occupied Little Round Top, three Alabama and two Texas regiments rushed in to seize the hill. The Forty-Seventh and

Fifteenth Alabama charged up its southern slope, meeting heavy resistance from Union troops positioned behind low stone walls above them. Then, under the command of Joshua Lawrence Chamberlain, the men of the Twentieth Maine fixed their bayonets and screamed down Little Round Top. The sight unnerved the Confederates, who retreated in disorder.

By sunset, the fighting south of the town of Gettysburg had died down. The Union regiments retreated to Cemetery Ridge to the south, while Longstreet's Confederates pulled back to the west. The murderous fighting had killed or wounded thousands of Union and Confederate soldiers. Just a few hundred yards of ground had been gained by the Southerners. However, Jeb Stuart's cavalry had finally reached the outskirts of Gettysburg in the late afternoon of July 2.

AT THE WEIKERT FARM

By the second day of Gettysburg, most civilians had fled the town. Seeking safety, Jacob Weikert left his small farm near Little Round Top. He returned just after the battle. Dozens of men lay dead and wounded on his property. Many of the wounded had been brought directly into Weikert's home. There, surgeons and nurses had been hard at work throughout the night. The yard was a scene of horror, with several fresh graves and piles of amputated limbs. The Weikerts found their furniture and belongings undisturbed. But strangely, they were missing a large parlor rug. The mystery was solved later, when the graves in their yard were dug up. The gravediggers had torn the rug into strips to use as shrouds for the dead.

His troops would be vital for the fighting that lay ahead. General Lee as well as General Meade held their ground and prepared for another day of battle.

Union troops held Little Round Top after the second day of fighting.

JEB STUART

1833–1864

As did many Southerners in the US Army, James Ewell Brown "Jeb" Stuart resigned at the outbreak of the Civil War to join the Confederate forces. He was an experienced cavalryman, having fought against Native American tribes on the western frontier.

Stuart was known for carrying out surprise cavalry raids. He led units over long distances, swooping down and scattering Union troops from their positions far from the front lines. His reputation earned him a promotion to commander of cavalry for the Army of Northern Virginia in 1862. During the Gettysburg campaign, Stuart's talent for long-range missions did not help General Lee. For several crucial days, Stuart's cavalry was out of touch with Lee. The Confederate cavalry only joined the battle late on the second day. Its route to the battle was blocked by Union horsemen under the command of General George Armstrong Custer.

It was traditional for cavalry commanders to fight alongside their men. In 1864, this habit cost Stuart his life. On May 11, Stuart was hit in the abdomen by a Union sharpshooter's bullet. He died the next day.

Culp's Hill was a valuable military position.

CHAPTER
★ 7 ★

PICKETT'S CHARGE

In the early morning hours of July 3, Confederate scouts at the northern end of the Gettysburg battlefield could hear movement, noise, and low talking coming from Culp's Hill. The Union troops had hauled artillery pieces to the top of the hill to fortify their position. Grumbling with the effort, they had moved large stones and heavy branches in place to create a defensive works.

Meade wanted to hold Culp's Hill, Cemetery Ridge, and Little Round Top at all costs. The troops between these northern and southern ridges were arranged so they could quickly move to help other units. Taking advantage of his strong position, Meade moved the I and VI Corps north to reinforce the XII Corps. To win the battle, the Confederate army would need to attack the high ground, overrun the Union positions, and disrupt Meade's supply line running south along the Baltimore Road.

Confederate General Ewell's corps had advanced to the thickly forested lower slopes of Culp's Hill overnight. The big Union guns were in place, waiting. Shortly after dawn, these guns opened up on the Confederates. Skirmishers from both sides advanced, trading shots across the wooded northern slopes. Trees were sliced in half by bullets and shells. A rain of branches fell on the troops below, along with flocks of dead birds that had been shot out of the trees.

The noise of rifle volleys and cannons boomed across the ridges and over the fields surrounding Gettysburg. In town, terrified civilians again took to their cellars, fearful the battle was coming back to their streets.

The battle for Culp's Hill lasted eight hard-fought hours. Wave after wave of Confederate infantry struggled up the slopes, only to be met by devastating volleys from the Twenty-Eighth Pennsylvania, the Seventy-Eighth New York, and other Union regiments.

A CIVILIAN CASUALTY

The noise of rifles and heavy artillery thundered over Gettysburg for three days. Civilians caught in the town took shelter in their homes. Those who had underground cellars made use of them. Twenty-year-old Mary "Ginnie" Wade and her sister waited out the battle in a small, one-story house. While working in the kitchen on July 3, a bullet passed through two doors of the house and struck Ginnie in the back. She died immediately, the only civilian casualty in the Battle of Gettysburg.

Union artillery became part of a memorial on Culp's Hill honoring Gettysburg veterans.

At midday, the Union forced Ewell's exhausted troops off the heights and back north.

Lee's army could no longer outflank the Union army on the north end of the battlefield. Union guns commanded the lowlands surrounding Culp's Hill, as well as the land west of Cemetery Hill. But the Confederates were strongest farther south. In this rolling farmland, crisscrossed by fences and roads, they still had a chance to concentrate their forces and defeat Meade's army.

LONGSTREET AND LEE DISAGREE

Union guns and infantry fortified the northern end of the Gettysburg battlefield. After the heavy fighting of July 2, the Northerners also held Little Round Top, which lay south of Cemetery Ridge. General Lee realized Meade must have moved troops from the center to reinforce his line at the northern end of the battlefield. The Union line was now weakest where the Confederates were strong—in the fields facing the southern reaches of the ridge. He was convinced his army's best chance for victory was to attack in force and break this portion of the Union front.

On the afternoon of July 3, Lee ordered Longstreet's corps and six brigades of A. P. Hill's corps across one mile (1.6 km) of open field against the Union center. The Confederates would bring approximately 15,000 men to this attack—an immense wave of infantry.[1] Lee believed the battle-hardened Southerners would succeed against a short stretch of thin Union defenses. He hoped a massive artillery bombardment before the advance would soften up the Union lines.

But General Longstreet was not happy with Lee's plan. Studying the ground ahead and the Union defenses, he saw very little chance of success. His troops would have to cross open ground in full view of the enemy guns. Those who survived would find themselves at the base of Cemetery Ridge, still under fire. They would then have to fight uphill to dislodge the Union troops, many of whom had been dug in for two days.

Longstreet could not convince Lee of the dangers, however. The two men were on friendly terms, but Longstreet and Lee had very different approaches to battlefield tactics. While Lee took risks and moved aggressively, Longstreet was cautious. He favored well-protected, defensive positions. But Longstreet greatly

LONGSTREET'S CONTROVERSIAL LEGACY

While Robert E. Lee remains a revered hero in the South, General Longstreet's legacy is more controversial. Some historians believe Longstreet's opposition to Lee's battle plan at Gettysburg helped bring about the Confederates' defeat. After the war, Longstreet worked for the federal government as postmaster of Gainesville, Georgia, and as ambassador to the Ottoman Empire. His work for the US government aroused hard feelings among former Confederates in the South, as did his support for Union general Ulysses S. Grant in the 1868 presidential election. Three years prior, General Grant had accepted General Lee's surrender at the end of the Civil War.

respected Lee for the many victories the Confederate general had won. He would follow Lee's orders, though without enthusiasm.

THE LAST CHARGE

Longstreet ordered his division commanders to form up their lines facing the open ground west of Cemetery Ridge. There was considerable confusion as the Confederate regiments maneuvered into place. Many of them had lost commanders and hundreds of enlisted men in the previous days' battles.

Seeing what lay ahead, Lieutenant James Crocker of the Ninth Virginia recalled, "All fully saw and appreciated the cost and the fearful magnitude of the assault, yet all were firmly resolved, if possible, to pluck victory from the very jaws of death itself."[2] A division under the command of General George E. Pickett was one of the last to join the front ranks. The 5,500 men in Pickett's division had marched 30 miles (48 km) the day before and encamped 4 miles (6.4 km) from the field where they now assembled.[3]

As Lee had planned, the Confederates began the assault with a massive artillery bombardment. Union guns answered with brisk firing. Neither bombardment was very effective. Most of the Confederate gunners overshot their targets on Cemetery Ridge. Union guns were also unable to thin out the ranks of Confederate infantry.

The sound and fury of the competing bombardments was intense. The ground shook as if an earthquake was taking place. The fearsome noise left many of the gunners temporarily deaf. The artillery thunder could be heard as far away as Philadelphia, more than 110 miles (177 km) to the east.

At approximately three in the afternoon, as ammunition on both sides dwindled, firing began to subside. Confederate officers prepared their infantry. The signal to advance would be a pair of artillery shots timed closely together. Pickett stayed behind with the other divisional commanders to watch from horseback. He was confident the Confederate army would succeed in breaking the Union lines. But they would have to be quick. The more time they spent in the open, the more men the army would lose.

In the afternoon heat, a sweeping line of Confederate soldiers marched quickly along a road lined with rail fences. Under a hail of shot and shell from Union artillery, the men struggled to take down the fences. Some simply climbed over them,

BIGGER CHARGE, BETTER RESULT

Pickett's Charge became the most famous cavalry charge of the Civil War. Approximately 15,000 Confederate troops took part, suffering tremendous casualties when Union guns and infantry forced them back with heavy casualties.[4] But Pickett's Charge was not the largest charge of the war. The Battle of Gaines Mill took place a year before the Battle of Gettysburg. The fighting occurred near Richmond, Virginia, the Confederate capital, and dragged on for a full day. Finally, at seven in the evening, Lee ordered his entire army to advance on the Union lines. The massive charge drove the Union lines back, and the Confederates won the day.

but these men trying to jump the fence made easy targets for Union rifles. Once the Confederates reached the far side of the road, they were battered by canister shot, which exploded into hundreds of small, razor-sharp fragments. The Union troops rained down a hail of bullets from behind stone walls on the slopes of Cemetery Ridge.

Men were falling all along the front lines of Pickett's division. "Many a poor fellow thought his time had come," recalled one veteran of the charge. "Great big, stout-hearted men prayed—loudly, too."[5] The Confederates continued their advance. Several regiments reached the base of Cemetery Ridge and managed to fight through breaches in the walls. Union rifles blasted great gaps in the Confederate line, and where the two sides met, ferocious hand-to-hand combat took place. Smoke from the artillery blasts began to shroud the battlefield. Hundreds of dead and wounded soon littered the ground.

After more than 50 percent of Pickett's men were killed or wounded, the division faltered and broke apart, along with other units in the assault.[6] The Confederates were forced to fall back. "Pickett's Charge," as historians call it, had failed, and the final battle of Gettysburg was lost.

LEE'S LAST ATTEMPT AT VICTORY

Lee ordered Jeb Stuart to bring his cavalry up from the east. Lee hoped doing so would bring overwhelming force against the Union troops. But Stuart's men were

GEORGE E. PICKETT

1825–1875

The son of a proud Virginia family, George Pickett did not much care for school. He finished last in his class of 1846 at West Point. Nevertheless, he won fame during the Mexican-American War (1846–1848) by bravely carrying the US flag to the roof of enemy headquarters during the Battle of Chapultepec.

On the third day of Gettysburg, Lee ordered Pickett to advance his division across open fields toward Cemetery Ridge. Pickett watched intently from the rear, cutting an impressive figure atop his horse. He wore fine clothes and kept his hair long and flowing. Though Pickett did not plan the bloody and futile assault, historians call the failed attack "Pickett's Charge." After the war, he settled in Norfolk, Virginia, where he worked as an insurance agent. When asked to explain the Confederate defeat at Gettysburg, his customary reply was, "I always thought the Yankees had something to do with it."[7]

On July 3, 1863, the Battle of Gettysburg came to a bloody close.

bone-weary after several days of riding behind enemy lines. Several brigades of Michigan cavalry met the Confederate horsemen and blocked their advance. This failure and the overwhelming artillery and infantry fire pouring into the Confederate lines forced Longstreet's and Hill's troops to finally retreat.

Pickett's own division was decimated. Lee held his troops in position, prepared for a counterattack on July 4. His last hope was that Meade would rush his troops to advance, exposing them to a flanking attack by the Confederates.

But the Union counterattack never took place. Aware of Lee's talent for defeating armies much larger than his own, cautious General Meade held his troops in place. With all hopes of outmaneuvering and breaking the Army of the Potomac now gone, Lee was forced to lead his army out of Pennsylvania. A total of 51,112 men on both sides were now dead, wounded, or missing.[8] The Confederate invasion of the North had come to a bloody, unsuccessful end.

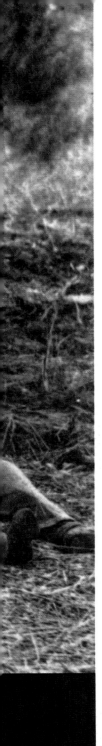

CHAPTER
8

AFTERMATH

Two wounded armies woke on the morning of July 4 across the bloodiest battlefield of the Civil War, or any war fought on American soil. Union troops still held Cemetery Ridge, Little Round Top, and Culp's Hill. But they were not coming after the Confederate army. Surveying the battlefield, Lee realized his army could not muster enough men or guns for another attack. Nor could it dig in and fight an extended campaign. Supplies were running low, and the fields of Gettysburg could provide no more food for the men or fodder for the horses. There was nothing more the battered Confederate army could accomplish, and by trying to outmaneuver Meade through another day of battle, Lee would risk total destruction of the Confederate forces.

GRIM DUTY

S. R. Norris of the Seventh Ohio was one soldier given the grim duty of burying the dead. "As long as reason holds her sway, I shall remember that day and its ghastly dead," he wrote. "We took them from perfect lines of battle as they had fallen; we dragged them out from behind rocks; we found them behind logs or lying over them, with eyes and mouths distended, and faces blackened by mortification. We found them everywhere in our front, from within a few feet of our fortifications to the foot of the hill."[1]

BOTH ARMIES RETREAT

The roads out of Gettysburg had grown slippery with mud and streaming water from rains the night before. General Meade had an important decision to make. If he pursued Lee, he had a chance to follow up the battle at Gettysburg with another fight that could chase the Confederates all the way to Richmond.

But Meade was cautious and wary of Lee's aggressive tactics. The Union army had been fighting for three days. For now, he would only ask his soldiers to march. They set out on July 5 and headed south to Frederick, Maryland. Meade followed Lee's forces but avoided any fighting, and his army stayed in Union territory north of the Potomac River.

Meade's decision angered President Lincoln. Once again, as at the Battle of Antietam the year before, the Confederate army was being allowed to slip away after a defeat. The president drafted a letter to Meade, saying: "I do not believe you appreciate the magnitude of the misfortune involved in Lee's escape. He was within your easy grasp, and to have closed upon him would, in connection with our other late successes, have ended the war."[2]

Lincoln decided not to send the letter. He may have realized that after three days of fighting, Meade's army was in no condition to pursue Lee and fight another major battle. Though he thought Meade too cautious, Lincoln gave the general credit for outsmarting Lee on the battlefield and preserving the Army of the Potomac. Meade continued to serve as a Union general.

On the Confederate side, wagons carrying the wounded would take a separate route from the main army. If Meade caught able-bodied Confederate regiments mingled with the wagons, Lee realized his army would have very little chance to escape.

GETTYSBURG BECOMES A MONUMENT

After the Battle of Gettysburg, two local attorneys formed an association to preserve the battlefield. They began buying plots of land where the fighting had taken place. Since that time, Gettysburg has become a national military park, with more than 1,300 monuments as well as museums, plaques, walking trails, and observation towers.[3]

Lee placed Brigadier General John Imboden in command of the column of approximately 1,200 wagons.[4] It stretched for 17 miles (27.4 km) along Maryland's roads toward Virginia. The Confederate cavalry brigades rode west through Cashtown and then south to screen the infantry column, which marched directly south for the Potomac River. The crossing, which was done using rafts

Pickett led thousands of men into battle for Pickett's Charge.

and ferries, was dangerous. The river had swollen with heavy rains in the days preceding the battle.

The defeat at Gettysburg was a harsh blow for Lee, and the failure of Pickett's Charge haunted the general for the rest of his life. Visiting Longstreet's tent after the battle, Lee took the blame on himself. "It's all my fault," he told Longstreet. "I thought my men were invincible."[5]

Placing responsibility for the defeat has been a hot subject among historians ever since. Many Civil War historians blame Longstreet for not following Lee's directions on the second day of battle, when Lee sought to turn the Union flank on Cemetery Ridge. Others fault Ewell for not attacking Culp's Hill late on the first day, or Stuart for disappearing with his cavalry until the afternoon of July 2. Others put the blame on Lee for ordering Pickett's Charge, which had little chance of success.

Students of the battle also point out Meade's capable handling of the Union army. At the time of Gettysburg, Meade had been in command for less than a week. Several of his commanders—including Reynolds, Hancock, and Sickles—had a dangerous habit of making decisions on their own. Nevertheless, Meade skillfully positioned his army on Cemetery Ridge and prepared his forces well for the Confederate onslaught on the last day of the battle.

Shortly after the battle, General Lee offered his resignation to Jefferson Davis, the president of the Confederacy. Having no other commander with Lee's ability and stature among the troops, Davis turned him down. Lee remained the commander of the Army of Northern Virginia until his surrender to General Grant at Appomattox Court House, Virginia, on April 9, 1865.

TENDING THE WOUNDED

At the end of the battle, Union and Confederate dead, wounded, or missing totaled 51,112.[6] Soldiers were assigned to bury men whom they had been fighting the day before. Thousands of wounded would die over the following weeks from infection, loss of blood, or shock. Some lay helpless in the open fields, while others were moved to homes, barns, and sheds in and around Gettysburg. Military surgeons worked in private homes or field hospitals set up in tents. Using heavy bone saws, they amputated arms and legs damaged by bullets or shrapnel. They had to work fast. A serious condition called gangrene could kill a man within a day. Soldiers acquired gangrene, the death of tissue, after an injury reduced blood flow to a part of the body. For anesthesia, they used the chemicals ether or chloroform, if they had them available, or whiskey.

In the operating rooms, Union and Confederate troops lay side by side. Leaving the battlefield, the Confederate army could not set up field hospitals for its own wounded. Some were placed on wagons to join the Confederate retreat. Others were left behind. If they could not walk, they were stranded where they fell. If they were not found and brought to a hospital, they died where they lay.

THE GRIM HARVEST

The fields around Gettysburg had been transformed into ghastly open graveyards. More than 7,000 bodies littered the ground, quickly decomposing in the July heat.[7] On the day after the battle, one Confederate soldier recorded the scene:

> *The sights and smells that assailed us were simply indescribable—corpses swollen to twice their size, asunder with the pressure of gases and vapors. . . . The odors were nauseating, and so deadly that in a short time we all sickened and were lying with our mouths close to the ground, most of us vomiting profusely.*[8]

Over the next few days, hundreds of men were buried together in mass graves. Some could be identified, but many could not. The armies of the Civil War provided no identification papers or dog tags for their soldiers. As a result, their deaths could not be confirmed, and approximately 11,000 soldiers were reported missing.[9]

After Gettysburg, the state of Pennsylvania bought land adjoining the Evergreen Cemetery, which had inspired the name for Cemetery Hill, and established the Gettysburg National Cemetery. In November 1863, workers exhumed more than 3,500 Union soldiers from their temporary graves around Gettysburg and moved them to the hill.[10]

A piece of artillery overlooks graves at Gettysburg National Cemetery.

On November 19, a dedication ceremony took place at the new cemetery. The main speaker was Edward Everett, a renowned orator, pastor, and politician from Massachusetts. President Lincoln was also invited to give a few words. Knowing Everett would give a long speech, the president kept his words brief, working on several drafts in the days leading up the event.

A HARVEST OF DEATH

Gettysburg was not the first battlefield to be photographed in the days after the battle had ended. That distinction belonged to Antietam, which took place in western Maryland in September 1862. But the shocking results of three days of warfare on the once-peaceful fields surrounding Gettysburg were the subject of some of the war's most famous images.

On July 4, photographer Timothy O'Sullivan walked the battlefield, no more than a day after the retreat by General Lee. Hundreds of corpses remained unburied, and O'Sullivan chose to record the aftermath on an open, featureless field. The image, named *A Harvest of Death*, was featured in Gardner's collection of Civil War photographs, published in 1865. Under the photograph ran a caption. It opened: "Slowly, over the misty fields of Gettysburg . . . came the sunless morn, after the retreat by Lee's broken army. Through the shadowy vapors, it was, indeed, a 'harvest of death' that was presented; hundreds and thousands of torn Union and rebel soldiers . . . strewed the now quiet fighting ground, soaked by the rain, which for two days had drenched the country with its fitful showers."[11]

Timothy O'Sullivan's iconic image *A Harvest of Death*

Lincoln was right about Everett, whose description of the battle went on for nearly two hours. Rousing applause was the crowd's answer, followed by respectful silence as the president walked to the podium. Then, in the course of two minutes, Lincoln gave a speech of 272 words. His Gettysburg Address was so short that the audience was taken aback when it abruptly ended.

Lincoln gave this speech in the middle of the Civil War. He had no way of knowing the war would last another 17 months, or that it would result in a Union victory. He mentioned the founding fathers and their struggle to establish a government dedicated to liberty and equality. He also spoke of the sacrifice of the Union soldiers who died at Gettysburg. They must not die in vain, Lincoln said, and the struggle for the Union must continue, so that "government of the people, by the people, for the people, shall not perish from the earth."[12]

GETTYSBURG'S LEGACY

Both sides entered the Civil War with hope for a swift and glorious victory. By the Battle of Gettysburg, it had become a disaster that touched millions of families, many of whom lost their homes, their livelihoods, and their sons, brothers, and fathers. For the people and soldiers of the North, Lincoln's Gettysburg Address gave meaning to the many hardships of the war and evidence that the cause of the Union was just.

The battle itself ended any hope Lee and the Confederate army had of bringing the war to Northern soil and persuading Lincoln's government to come to terms. When the Mississippi River town of Vicksburg, Mississippi, fell to the Union army on July 4, the Confederacy also lost access to the river as a supply route and to easy communication with western states such as Arkansas and Texas. General Grant gained a useful base for further assaults on Confederate strongholds, putting the Confederate army in the west on the defensive. There would be almost two more years of fighting, but Gettysburg and Vicksburg had turned the tide of the war in favor of the Union army.

LIVING HISTORY

Every year, thousands of people gather at Gettysburg to reenact the battle. Anyone can apply to play the part of a soldier or civilian. The standards for battle reenactors are strict. They must wear period uniforms, sleep in tents, and use authentic weapons to bring the scene alive. They may not wear sneakers, modern shoes, or glasses with plastic frames. Nor may they do impressions of important figures such as General Lee or General Meade without permission. Park visitors can watch the reenactment. They are treated to artillery and cavalry demonstrations, mock battles, dances, religious revival meetings, and concerts. A battlefield guide narrates the events as they unfold.

THE GETTYSBURG ADDRESS

President Lincoln's address at the dedication of the Gettysburg National Cemetery was just 272 words long. Though brief, Lincoln's speech had a powerful effect on his audience. The day after the dedication, Edward Everett wrote Lincoln a letter in admiration. He wrote, "I should be glad, if I could flatter myself that I came as near to the central idea of the occasion, in two hours, as you did in two minutes."[13] At the dedication, his short speech was:

> Fourscore and seven years ago our fathers brought forth on this continent a new nation, conceived in liberty and dedicated to the proposition that all men are created equal. Now we are engaged in a great civil war, testing whether that nation or any nation so conceived and so dedicated can long endure. We are met on a great battlefield of that war. We have come to dedicate a portion of that field as a final resting-place for those who here gave their lives that that nation might live. It is altogether fitting and proper that we should do this. But in a larger sense, we cannot dedicate, we cannot consecrate, we cannot hallow this ground. The brave men, living and dead who struggled here have consecrated it far above our poor power to add or detract. The world will little note nor long remember what we say here, but it can never forget what they did here. It is for us the living, rather, to be dedicated here to the unfinished work which they who fought here have thus far so nobly advanced. It is rather for us to be here dedicated to the great task remaining before us—that from these honored dead we take increased devotion to that cause for which they gave the last full measure of devotion—that we here highly resolve that these dead shall not have died in vain--that this nation under God shall have a new birth of freedom, and that government of the people, by the people, for the people shall not perish from the earth.[14]

President Lincoln, *circled*, gave his 272-word Gettysburg Address on November 19, 1863.

TIMELINE

November 6, 1860

Abraham Lincoln wins the US presidential election.

December 20, 1860

South Carolina declares its secession from the United States.

February 1, 1861

Six other states join South Carolina in seceding from the United States.

April 12, 1861

Confederate batteries open fire on Fort Sumter in the harbor of Charleston, South Carolina.

June 28, 1863

President Lincoln promotes General George Meade as the new commander of the Army of the Potomac.

July 1, 1863

Confederate and Union infantry clash just west of Gettysburg on Seminary Ridge.

July 2, 1863

Union troops and artillery stop Confederate assaults on Cemetery Ridge and Little Round Top.

July 3, 1863

Union troops stop Pickett's Charge in the fields and hills west of Cemetery Ridge, ending the Battle of Gettysburg.

September 17, 1862

Union and Confederate armies clash at the Battle of Antietam.

May 3, 1863

A Union army under General Oliver Howard is outflanked and defeated at Chancellorsville, Virginia.

June 15, 1863

General Robert E. Lee leads the Army of Northern Virginia across the Potomac River and north into Maryland.

June 26, 1863

General Ewell's corps occupies the town of Gettysburg before pushing east to the Susquehanna River.

July 4, 1863

General Lee orders his army to retreat back across the Potomac to Virginia.

July 4, 1863

Photographer Timothy O'Sullivan immortalizes Gettysburg's dead in *A Harvest of Death.*

November 19, 1863

President Lincoln delivers the Gettysburg Address.

April 9, 1865

The Confederate army formally surrenders at Appomattox Court House in Virginia, ending the Civil War.

ESSENTIAL FACTS

KEY PLAYERS

- US president Abraham Lincoln, after serving one term as a congressman from Illinois in the House of Representatives, returned to Washington after election as president in 1860.

- Union general George Gordon Meade, who served as a military and civilian engineer before the Civil War, rose steadily as an officer in the Union army before his appointment by President Lincoln as commander of the Army of the Potomac just three days before the Battle of Gettysburg.

- Confederate general Robert E. Lee, renowned for his aggressive tactics at the Battle of Chancellorsville, marched his army north into Pennsylvania in June 1863, seeking to wreak such destruction on the Union army that the US government would sue for peace.

- Confederate general James Longstreet, one of the most capable officers on either side of the Civil War, respectfully disagreed with Lee's plan for a full-scale assault on the third day of Gettysburg, and reluctantly led the doomed advance against a strong Union position.

CASUALTIES

- Dead: Union: 3,155; Confederate: 3,903

- Wounded: Union: 14,529; Confederate: 18,735

- Missing: Union: 5,365; Confederate: 5,425

- Total: Union: 23,049; Confederate: 28,063

IMPACT ON WAR

The Battle of Gettysburg turned back the invasion of the North by General Robert E. Lee's Army of Northern Virginia. Lee's army regrouped in Virginia, and the war lasted for 21 more months. But Gettysburg was an important turning point, after which the Confederacy remained on the defensive until Lee's surrender in April 1865.

QUOTE

"It's all my fault. I thought my men were invincible."

—Confederate General Robert E. Lee on his loss at Gettysburg

GLOSSARY

ARTILLERY

A large gun manned by a crew of operators used to shoot long distances.

BRIGADE

A military unit made up of several regiments, and in some cases an attached cavalry squad and artillery batteries.

CAVALRY

A military unit consisting of soldiers mounted on horseback.

CIVILIAN

A person not serving in the armed forces.

CORPS

A large military unit consisting of several infantry divisions, in addition to artillery, cavalry, engineers, and supply units.

DEPLOY

To spread out strategically; to send into battle.

FLANKING

A battlefield maneuver in which one unit moves from the front to the sides or rear of an opponent, putting the opponent at a tactical disadvantage.

FRIENDLY FIRE
Weapon fire coming from one's own side.

GARRISON
A military camp, fort, or base.

INFANTRY
A group of soldiers trained and armed to fight on foot.

MILITIA
A military force made up of nonprofessional fighters.

PICKET
A group of soldiers standing guard.

RECONNAISSANCE
An exploration of an area to gather information about the activity of military forces.

REGIMENT
An army unit typically commanded by a colonel.

SKIRMISH
A minor battle between two groups of enemy troops.

ADDITIONAL RESOURCES

SELECTED BIBLIOGRAPHY

Foote, Shelby. *The Civil War: A Narrative.* Vol. 2. New York: Vintage, 1986. Print.

Guelzo, Allen C. *Gettysburg: The Last Invasion.* New York: Knopf, 2013. Print.

McPherson, James M. *Battle Cry of Freedom: The Civil War Era.* New York: Oxford UP, 1988. Print.

Sears, Stephen W. *Gettysburg.* Boston: Houghton Mifflin, 2003. Print.

FURTHER READINGS

Hamilton, John. *Battle of Gettysburg.* Minneapolis: Abdo, 2014. Print.

Martin, Iain C. *Gettysburg: The True Account of Two Young Heroes in the Greatest Battle of the Civil War.* New York: Sky Pony, 2013. Print.

Vansant, Wayne. *Gettysburg: The Graphic History of America's Most Famous Battle and the Turning Point of the Civil War.* Lake Forest, CA: Walter Foster, 2016. Print.

WEBSITES

To learn more about Essential Library of the Civil War, visit **booklinks.abdopublishing.com**. These links are routinely monitored and updated to provide the most current information available.

PLACES TO VISIT

Gettysburg Museum of History
219 Baltimore Street
Gettysburg, PA 17325
717-337-2035
https://www.gettysburgmuseumofhistory.com/
The Gettysburg Museum of History exhibits, buys, and sells a wide variety of artifacts, including weapons, flags, musical instruments, and other gear recovered from the Gettysburg battlefields and from other US wars.

Gettysburg National Military Park
1195 Baltimore Pike
Gettysburg, PA 17325-2804
717-334-1124
http://www.nps.gov/gett/index.htm
The largest Civil War battlefield monument, Gettysburg offers guided and self-guided walking tours, bike and horseback riding trails, and "living history" weekends, where you can talk with reenactors dressed in period costume. The David Wills house in the town of Gettysburg, where President Lincoln worked on the Gettysburg Address, appears as it did in 1863 and is open to visitors, as are many other homes in the area.

SOURCE NOTES

CHAPTER 1. FIGHTING ON SEMINARY RIDGE

1. Edward Longcare. *General John Buford: A Military Biography*. Cambridge, MA: Da Capo, 2003. Print. 192–193.

2. Richard Billies. "Jackson's Flank Attack: The Advance." *North against South: Understanding the American Civil War on Its 150th Anniversary*. North against South, 14 Jan. 2013. Web. 5 Feb. 2016.

CHAPTER 2. THE INVASION OF PENNSYLVANIA

1. Joseph E. Stevens. *1863: The Rebirth of a Nation*. New York: Bantam, 1999. Print. 226.

2. Earl J. Hess. "The Terrain and Fortifications of Harpers Ferry: September 12–15, 1862." *Harpers Ferry*. Civil War Trust, n.d. Web. 5 Feb. 2016.

3. Joseph E. Stevens. *1863: The Rebirth of a Nation*. New York: Bantam, 1999. Print. 227.

4. Shelby Foote. *The Civil War: A Narrative*. Vol. 2. New York: Vintage, 1986. Print. 443.

5. Michael Korda. *Clouds of Glory: The Life and Legend of Robert E. Lee*. New York: Harper, 2014. Print. 548.

6. "Civil War Army Organization: Innovations, Opportunities, Challenges." *Civil War Trust*. Civil War Trust, n.d. Web. 5 Feb. 2016.

CHAPTER 3. THE CONFEDERATES ARRIVE

None.

CHAPTER 4. THE DAY BEFORE GETTYSBURG

1. "The Civil War by the Numbers." *American Experience: Death and the Civil War*. WGBH Educational Foundation, 2013. Web. 5 Feb. 2016.

2. Shelby Foote. *The Civil War: A Narrative*. Vol. 2. New York: Vintage, 1986. Print. 465.

3. Rebecca Beatrice Brooks. "Female Soldiers at the Battle of Gettysburg." *Civil War Saga*. Civil War Saga, 31 May 2012. Web. 5 Feb. 2016.

4. Shelby Foote. *The Civil War: A Narrative*. Vol. 2. New York: Vintage, 1986. Print. 466.

CHAPTER 5. THE FIRST DAY OF GETTYSBURG

1. Harry W. Pfanz. *Gettysburg—The First Day*. Raleigh, NC: U of North Carolina, 2011. Print. 53.

2. "'No Man Can Take Those Colors and Live': The Epic Battle between the 24th Michigan and 26th North Carolina at Gettysburg." *Gettysburg*. Civil War Trust, n.d. Web. 5 Feb. 2016.

3. Scott Bowden and Bill Ward. *Last Chance for Victory: Robert E. Lee and the Gettysburg Campaign*. Cambridge, MA: Da Capo, 2001. Print. 203.

4. Allen C. Guelzo. *Gettysburg: The Last Invasion*. New York: Knopf, 2013. Print. 203.

SOURCE NOTES
CONTINUED

CHAPTER 6. THE SECOND DAY OF BATTLE

1. Allen C. Guelzo. *Gettysburg: The Last Invasion*. New York: Knopf, 2013. Print. 245.

2. Maja Beckstrom. "Minnesota Civil War Regiment Charged into History at Gettysburg." *Twin Cities Pioneer Press*. Digital First Media, 2016. Web. 5 Feb. 2016.

3. Phillip Thomas Tucker. *Storming Little Round Top*. Cambridge, MA: Da Capo, 2002. Print. 205.

CHAPTER 7. PICKETT'S CHARGE

1. Shelby Foote. *The Civil War: A Narrative*. Vol. 2. New York: Vintage, 1986. Print. 529–530.

2. Allen C. Guelzo. *Gettysburg: The Last Invasion*. New York: Knopf, 2013. Print. 393–394.

3. Richard Rollins. *Pickett's Charge: Eyewitness Accounts at the Battle of Gettysburg*. Mechanicsburg, PA: Stackpole, 2005. Print. 73.

4. Robert C. Cheeks. "Pickett's Charge." *America's Civil War*. History Net, 2016. Web. 5 Feb. 2016.

5. Shelby Foote. *The Civil War: A Narrative*. Vol. 2. New York: Vintage, 1986. Print. 549.

6. Robert C. Cheeks. "Pickett's Charge." *America's Civil War*. History Net, 2016. Web. 5 Feb. 2016.

7. Ibid.

8. "Gettysburg." *Battlefields*. Civil War Trust, n.d. Web. 5 Feb. 2016.

CHAPTER 8. AFTERMATH

1. John M. Archer. *Culp's Hill at Gettysburg: "The Mountain Trembled . . . "* El Dorado Hills, CA: Savas, 2014. Print. 117.

2. Joel Achenbach. "Gettysburg: The Battle and Its Aftermath." *Health & Science*. Washington Post, 29 Apr. 2013. Web. 5 Feb. 2016.

3. "Frequently Asked Questions." *Gettysburg National Military Park*. National Park Service, n.d. Web. 5 Feb. 2016.

4. Steve French. *Imboden's Brigade in the Gettysburg Campaign*. Hedgesville, WV: Morgan Messenger, 2010. Print. 90.

5. Michael Korda. *Clouds of Glory: The Life and Legend of Robert E. Lee*. New York: Harper, 2014. Print. 601.

6. "Gettysburg Casualties (Battle Deaths at Gettysburg)." *America's Civil War*. History Net, 2016. Web. 5 Feb. 2016.

7. Clyde Bell. "What Happened to the Confederate Dead?" *Blog of Gettysburg National Military Park*. Blog of Gettysburg National Military Park, 26 July 2012. Web. 5 Feb. 2016.

8. Ibid.

9. "Gettysburg Casualties (Battle Deaths at Gettysburg)." *America's Civil War*. History Net, 2016. Web. 5 Feb. 2016.

10. Ibid.

11. "Plate 36." *Gardner's Photographic Sketch Book of the War*. Cornell University Library Division of Rare & Manuscript Collections, 2002. Web. 5 Feb. 2016.

12. "The Gettysburg Address." *Avalon Project*. Lillian Goldman Law Library, n.d. Web. 5 Feb. 2016.

13. "The Gettysburg Address." *Library of Congress*. USA.gov, n.d. Web. 19 Feb. 2016.

14. "The Gettysburg Address." *Avalon Project*. Lillian Goldman Law Library, n.d. Web. 5 Feb. 2016.

INDEX

ABOUT THE AUTHOR

Tom Streissguth is the author of more than 100 books of nonfiction for the school and library market and the founder of The Archive of American Journalism, a unique collection of historical journalism that is presenting long-neglected work of major American authors including Jack London, Stephen Crane, Lincoln Steffens, Nellie Bly, and Ambrose Bierce. He currently lives in Woodbury, Minnesota.

ABOUT THE CONSULTANT

Erik B. Alexander received his PhD from the University of Virginia and is currently an assistant professor in the Department of Historical Studies at Southern Illinois University, Edwardsville. Previously, he was research assistant professor and an assistant editor of the Papers of Andrew Jackson (v. 9, 2013) at the University of Tennessee, Knoxville. His research focuses on the nineteenth-century United States, with a focus on the Civil War, Reconstruction, and political history. He is currently finishing a book on Northern Democrats after the Civil War, titled *Revolution Forestalled: The North and Reconstruction, 1865–1877*.